WORLD CELEBRATIONS

KWANZAA

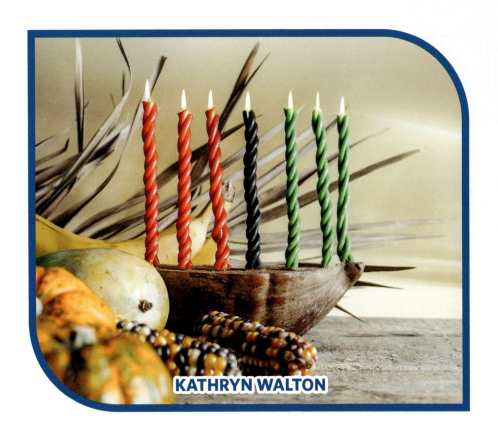

KATHRYN WALTON

Published in 2026 by The Rosen Publishing Group, Inc.
2544 Clinton Street, Buffalo, NY 14224

Copyright © 2026 by The Rosen Publishing Group, Inc.

All rights reserved. No part of this book may be reproduced in any form without permission in writing from the publisher, except by a reviewer.

First Edition

Editor: Greg Roza
Book Design: Rachel Rising

Photo Credits: Cover, p. 1 Shyntartanya/Shutterstock.com; pp. 4, 6, 8, 10, 12, 14, 16, 18, 20 Vjom/Shutterstock.com; pp. 5, 15, 17, 21 SeventyFour/Shutterstock.com; p. 7 Miaron Billy/Shutterstock.com; p. 9 https://commons.wikimedia.org/wiki/File:Kwanza-RonKarenga.jpg; pp. 11, 19 AnnaStills/Shutterstock.com; p. 13 Pixel-Shot/Shutterstock.com.

Some of the images in this book illustrate individuals who are models. The depictions do not imply actual situations or events.

Cataloging-in-Publication Data

Names: Walton, Kathryn, 1993-.
Title: Kwanzaa / Kathryn Walton.
Description: Buffalo, New York : PowerKids Press, 2026. | Series: World celebrations | Includes glossary and index.
Identifiers: ISBN 9781499452181 (pbk.) | ISBN 9781499452198 (library bound) | ISBN 9781499452204 (ebook)
Subjects: LCSH: Kwanzaa–Juvenile literature.
Classification: LCC GT4403.W367 2026 | DDC 394.2612–dc23

Manufactured in the United States of America

CPSIA Compliance Information: Batch #CSPK26. For Further Information contact Rosen Publishing at 1-800-237-9932.

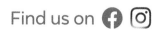

CONTENTS

African American Culture 4
First Fruit 6
Pan-African Celebration 8
The Seven Principles 10
Lighting Candles 12
Colorful Kwanzaa 14
Feast of Faith 16
Gift Giving 18
Around the World 20
Glossary 22
For More Infomation 23
Index. 24

African American Culture

Kwanzaa is one of the newest holidays in the world. It was first celebrated in 1966. It lasts from December 26 to January 1. Kwanzaa celebrates African American **culture**. People learn about African history and culture. Kwanzaa celebrations have colorful clothes, fun foods, music, and dancing!

First Fruit

The word "Kwanzaa" comes from *matunda ya Kwanzaa*. This is an African language called Swahili. It means "first fruit." This stands for the first fruits picked during a growing season. In Africa, people celebrate fruit **festivals** a few times a year.

Pan-African Celebration

Kwanzaa was created by a teacher named Maulana Karenga. He saw that most U.S. holidays were based on white, European culture. Karenga called Kwanzaa a "pan-African" celebration. This means it's a holiday for all Black people. Kwanzaa is a holiday that Black people can call their own.

The Seven Principles

Karenga based Kwanzaa on *Nguzo Saba*. This means Seven Principles. A principle is a basic rule or truth. Each day of Kwanzaa is based on one of the Seven Principles. The first day celebrates unity. This means togetherness. The seventh day celebrates faith in friends, family, and community.

Lighting Candles

The kinara is a candle holder. It holds one candle for each day of Kwanzaa. The candles are green, black, and red. Families light a new candle on each day of Kwanzaa. They talk about the principle for each day. On the last day, all seven candles are lit.

Colorful Kwanzaa

Families **decorate** their homes for Kwanzaa. Green, yellow, red, and black are the most common colors. These are thought of as pan-African colors. People wear colorful African clothing. Families put fruits and vegetables around the kinara. Corn stands for the children celebrating Kwanzaa!

Feast of Faith

A special meal is held on day six of Kwanzaa. This meal is called the Feast of Faith. Some people celebrate this day with family. Others join community feasts. These feasts have **traditional** African foods, music, and dancing. Families drink from a "unity cup" to honor their **ancestors**.

17

Gift Giving

Kwanzaa is a time for gift giving! Kids may receive fun treats. They also receive gifts that help celebrate Kwanzaa, such as books about the holiday. Some people like to make gifts for others. These can include colorful African clothes and handmade grass baskets.

Around the World

Kwanzaa was made for African Americans. However, it has become a celebration of African culture and Black people all over the world. But everyone can enjoy Kwanzaa! It is a holiday when everyone can learn and grow. Kwanzaa celebrations are also held in Canada, Jamaica, Brazil, and more!

21

GLOSSARY

ancestor: A person in your family who lived long before you.

culture: The beliefs and practices of a racial, religious, or social group.

decorate: To make something interesting or beautiful by adding things to it.

festival: A time of celebration in honor of something or someone special.

traditional: Having to do with the ways of doing things in a culture that are passed down from parents to children.

FOR MORE INFORMATION

BOOKS
Gobin, Shantel. *Kwanzaa*. Minneapolis, MN: Jump!, 2023.

Wing, Natasha, and Kristi Jewel. *The Night Before Kwanzaa*. New York, NY: Grosset & Dunlap, 2023.

WEBSITES

Celebrating Kwanzaa
kids.nationalgeographic.com/celebrations/article/Kwanzaaa
Read more about Kwanzaa in the United States as well as African culture.

Kwanzaa.org
kwanzaa.org
This resource for all things related to Kwanzaa includes a kids section with interactive games and puzzles.

Publisher's note to educators and parents: Our editors have carefully reviewed these websites to ensure that they are suitable for students. Many websites change frequently, however, and we cannot guarantee that a site's future contents will continue to meet our high standards of quality and educational value. Be advised that students should be closely supervised whenever they access the internet.

INDEX

A
Africa, 4, 6, 16, 18, 20

C
candles, 12
clothes, 4, 14, 18
culture, 4, 8, 20

F
family, 10, 12, 14, 16
Feast of Faith, 16
first fruit, 6
food, 4, 16

K
Karenga, Maulana, 8, 10
kinara, 12, 14

M
music and dancing, 4, 16

P
pan-African, 8, 14

S
Seven Principles, 10, 12